Pairs of People

by JEANNE & MARK K. SHRIVER

Illustrated by
LAURA WATSON

BOOKS & MEDIA
CHICAGO

4U2B
◀ BOOKS & MEDIA ▶

Text Copyright © 2022 Jeanne and Mark K. Shriver
Illustrations by Laura Watson Copyright © 2022 Loyola Press

Cover and interior design: Jill Arena
Cover art credit: Laura Watson

Interior art: Laura Watson
ISBN: 978-0-8294-5485-7
Library of Congress Control Number: 2022933933

The name of Best Buddies is reproduced with the kind permission of Best Buddies International, Inc. www.bestbuddies.org.

The name and mark of Save the Children is reproduced with the kind permission of Save the Children Federation, Inc. www.savethechildren.org.

The name and logo of SOME, So Others May Eat, is reproduced with their kind permission. www.some.org.

The name Special Olympics is reproduced with the kind permission of Special Olympics, Inc., Washington, DC, www.specialolympics.org, whose mission is to provide year-round sports training and athletic competition in a variety of Olympic-type sports for children and adults with intellectual disabilities, giving them continuing opportunities to develop physical fitness, demonstrate courage, experience joy, and participate in a sharing of gifts, skills, and friendship with their families, other Special Olympics athletes, and the community.

4U2B Books and Media is an imprint of Loyola Press,
8770 W. Bryn Mawr, Chicago, IL 60631   4U2BBooks.com

Printed in the United States of America.
22 23 24 25 26 27 28 29 30 31 CGC 10 9 8 7 6 5 4 3 2 1

TO LIBBY AND JOHN, EUNICE AND SARGE

Two wonderful pairs of people,
our fathers and mothers,
taught us the power of working together
in service to others.

1

One pair of people decides to work together. They help a neighbor clear the walk in the snowy weather.

1 Pair = 2 People

1 pair

2

Two pairs of people
see a dog in trouble.
They safely move her from the street.
Now the help is double.

2 Pairs = 4 People

1 pair

2 pairs

2 x 2 = 4

3

Three pairs of people can do a little more. They help their school custodian sweep and clean the floor.

3 Pairs = 6 People

 1 pair

 2 pairs

 3 pairs

5

Five pairs of people garden for endless hours, growing goodness for all to share, by planting veggies and flowers.

5 Pairs = 10 People

1 pair

2 pairs

3 pairs

4 pairs

5 pairs

6

Six pairs of people support civic connection. They spread the word all over town about this year's election.

6 Pairs = 12 People

1 pair | 2 pairs | 3 pairs | 4 pairs | 5 pairs | 6 pairs

7

Seven pairs of people offer hope for those in jail, raising money for some books at the village sale.

7 Pairs = 14 People

1 pair

2 pairs

3 pairs

4 pairs

5 pairs

6 pairs

8

Eight pairs of people work hard until it's dark. They support their community by tending the local park.

8 Pairs = 16 People

1 pair

2 pairs

3 pairs

4 pairs

5 pairs

6 pairs

$8 \times 2 = 16$

7 pairs **8 pairs**

9

Nine pairs of people know it's hard to live alone. They joyfully come together to fix their neighbor's home.

9 Pairs = 18 People

 1 pair
 2 pairs
 3 pairs
 4 pairs
 5 pairs
 6 pairs

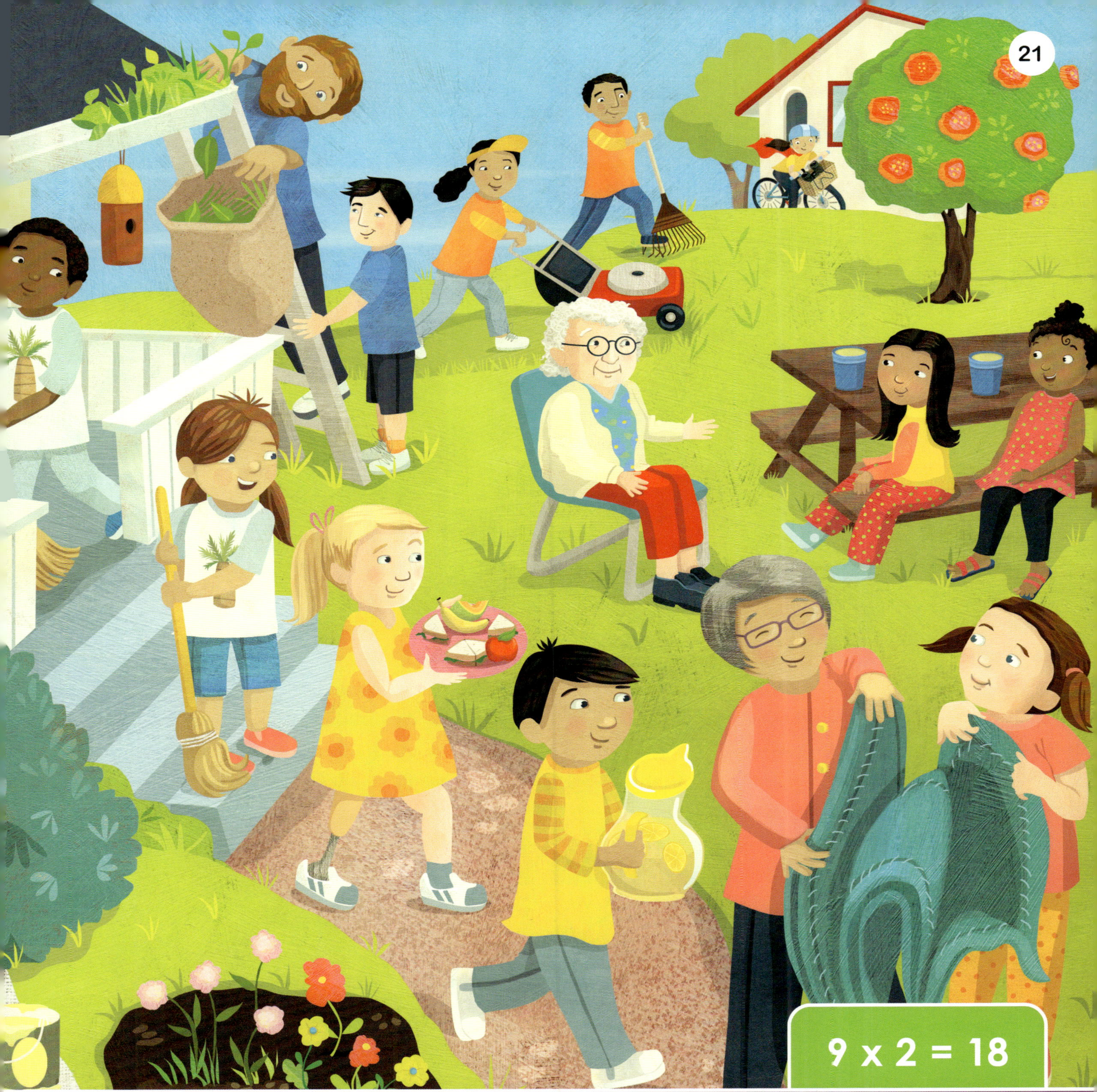

$9 \times 2 = 18$

7 pairs   8 pairs   9 pairs

10

Ten pairs of people help athletes keep the pace. They volunteer and celebrate at the Best Buddies race.

10 Pairs = 20 People

1 pair

2 pairs

3 pairs

4 pairs

5 pairs

6 pairs

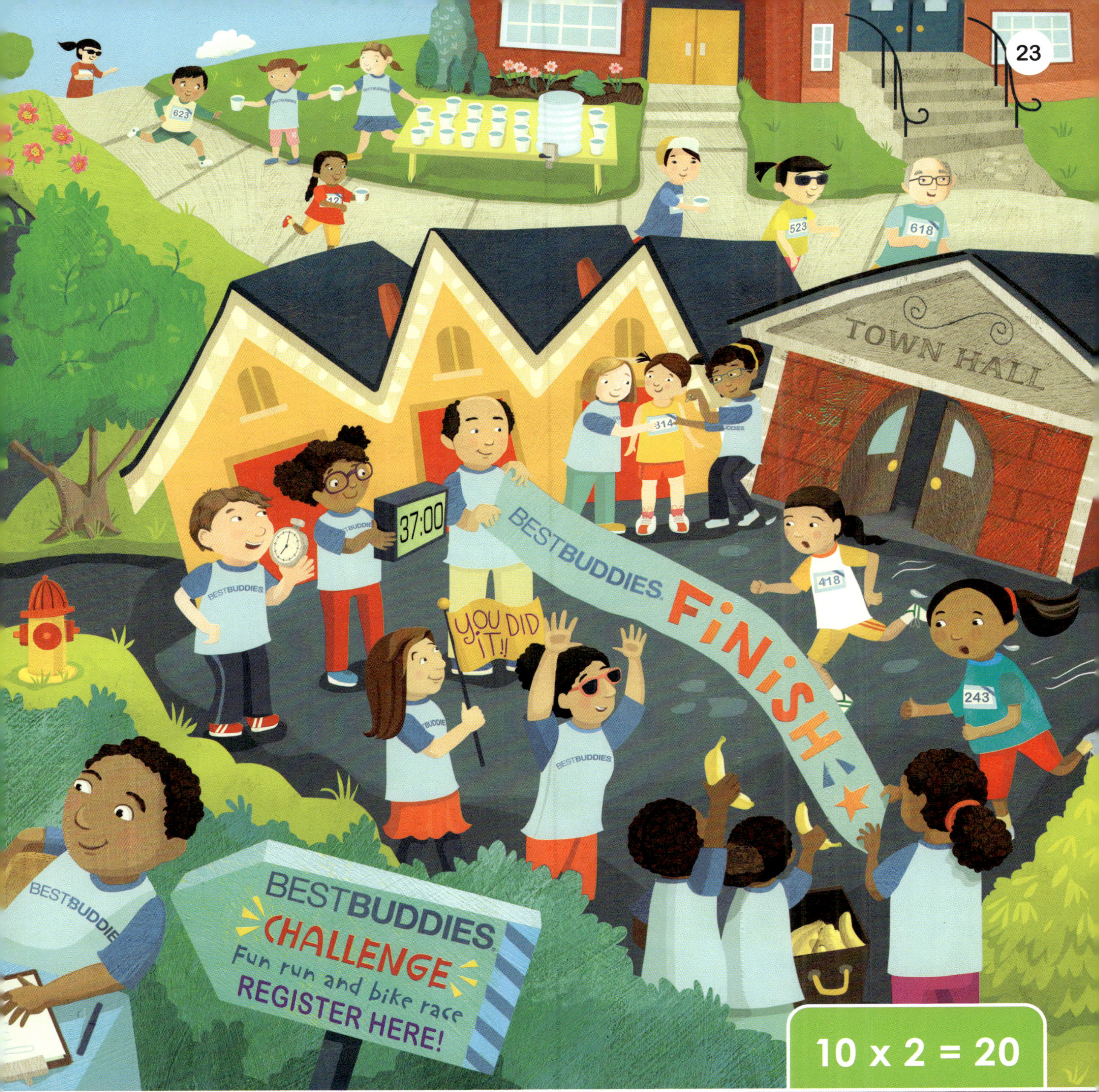

$10 \times 2 = 20$

 7 pairs

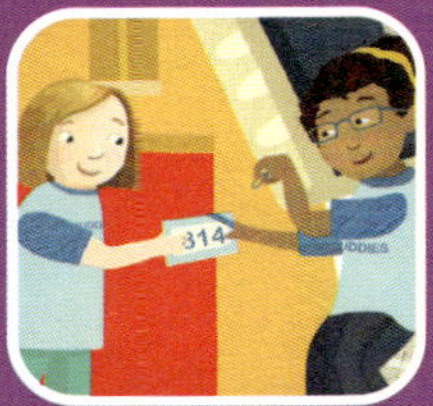

 8 pairs

 9 pairs

 10 pairs

11

Eleven pairs of people wade into the mud. They rescue friends and clean the mess from an unexpected flood.

11 Pairs = 22 People

1 pair   2 pairs   3 pairs   4 pairs   5 pairs   6 pairs

$11 \times 2 = 22$

7 pairs   8 pairs   9 pairs   10 pairs   11 pairs

So Others Migh[t]

12

Twelve pairs of people make meals for those in need. They like to work together so that everyone can succeed.

12 Pairs = 24 People

 1 pair
 2 pairs
 3 pairs
 4 pairs
 5 pairs
 6 pairs

Eat

27

12 × 2 = 24

7 pairs

8 pairs

9 pairs

10 pairs

11 pairs

12 pairs

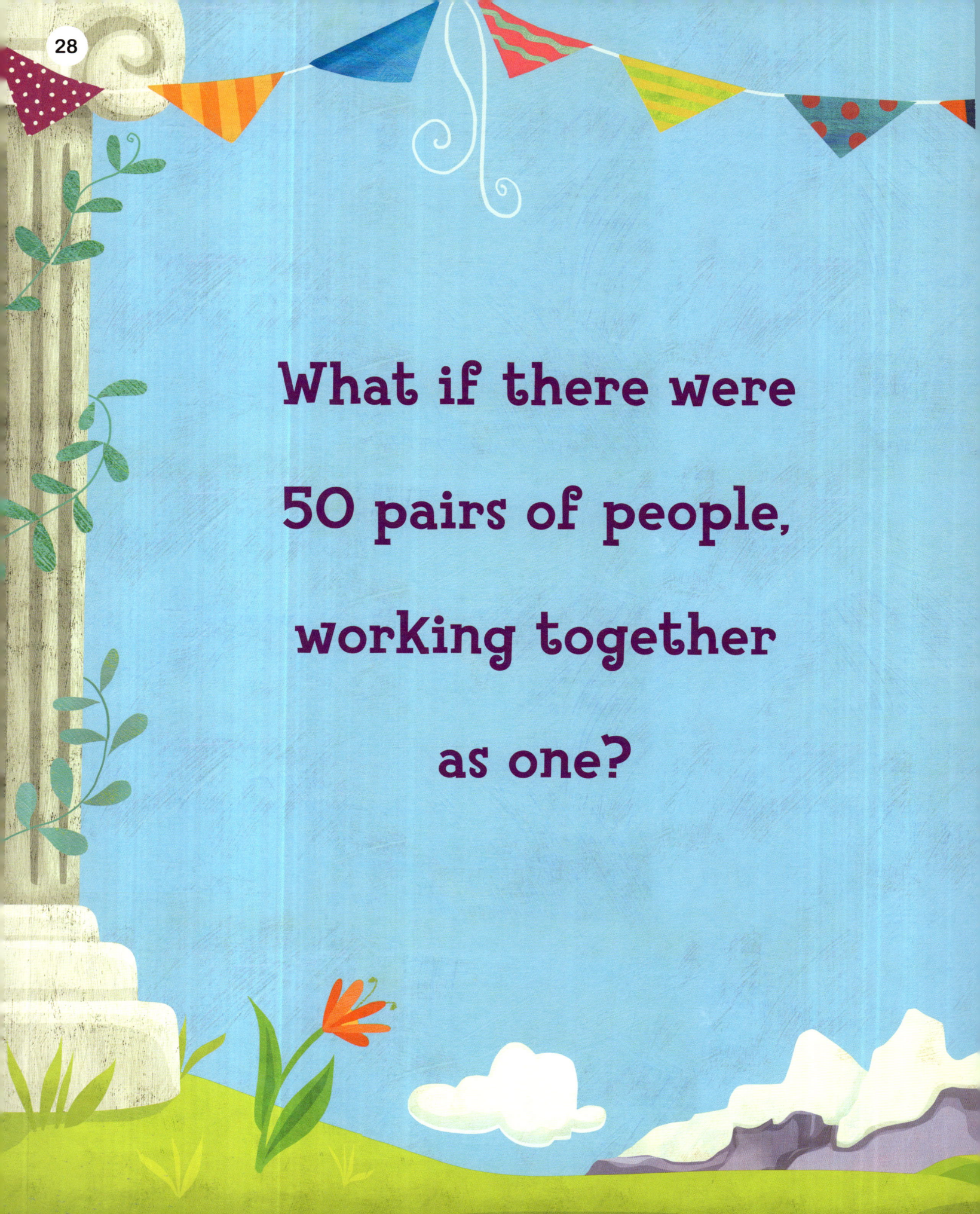

What if there were

50 pairs of people,

working together

as one?

What positive difference could they make? What goodness could be done?

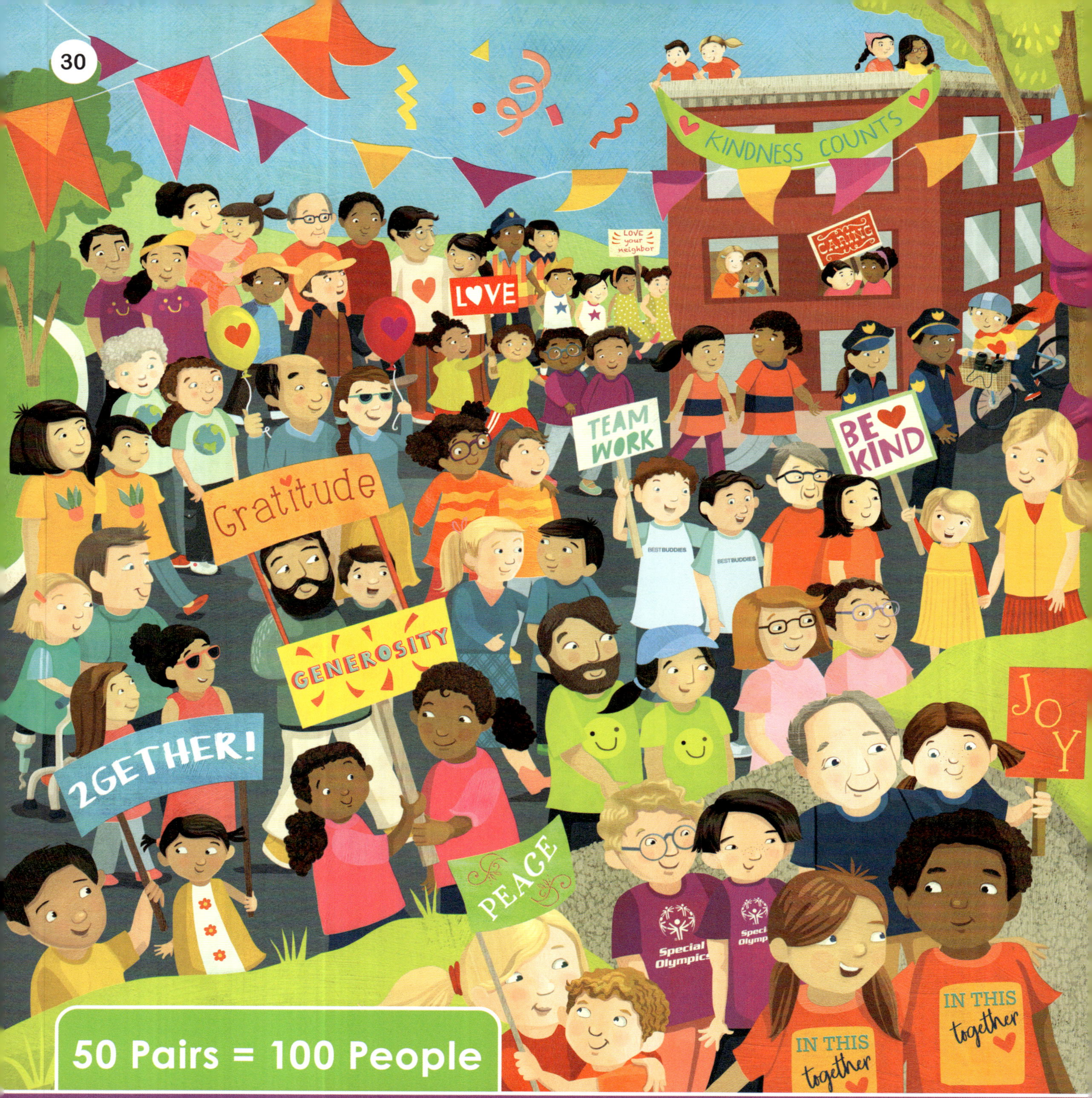

50 Pairs = 100 People

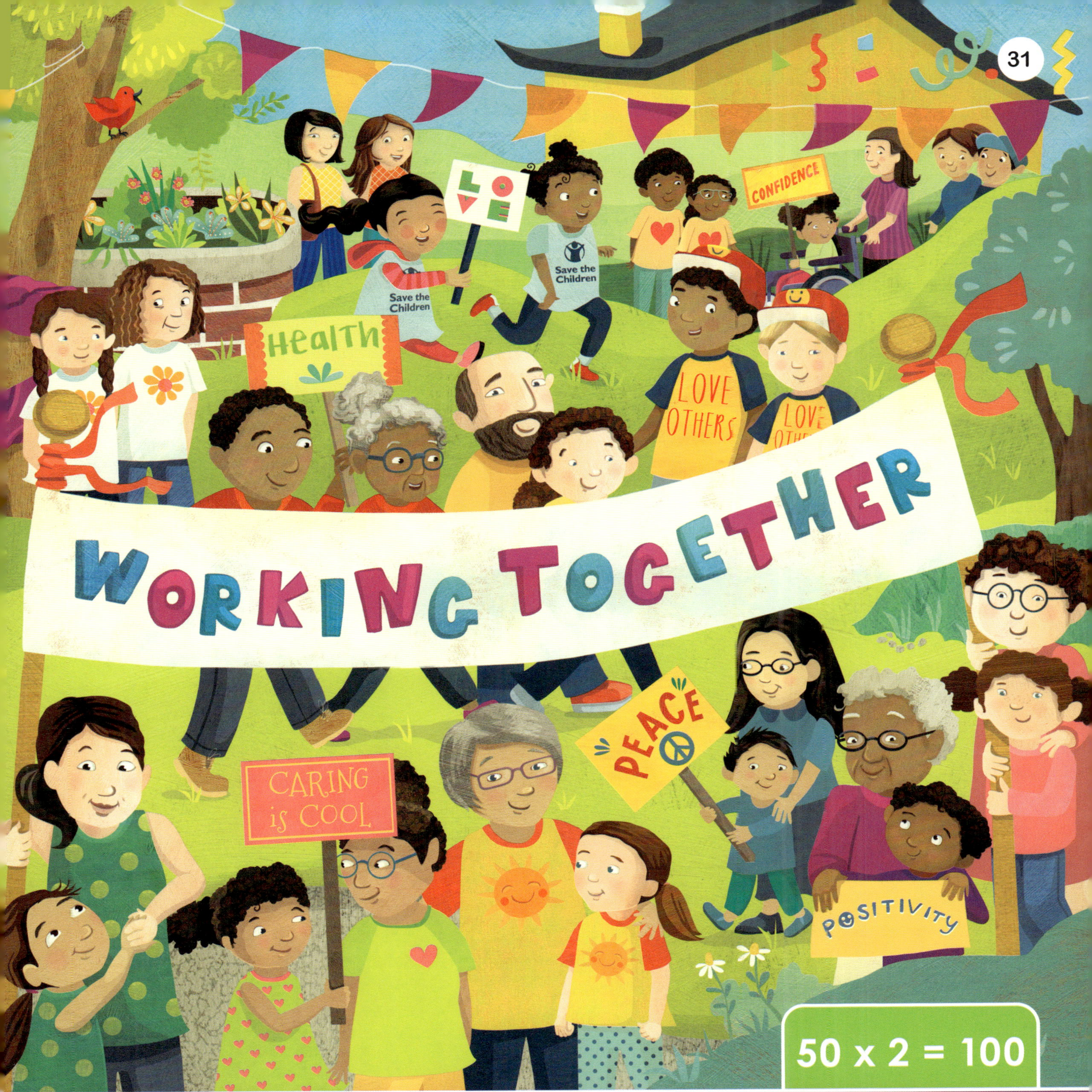
LOVE
Save the Children
Save the Children
CONFIDENCE
Health
LOVE OTHERS
WORKING TOGETHER
PEACE
CARING is COOL
POSITIVITY

50 x 2 = 100

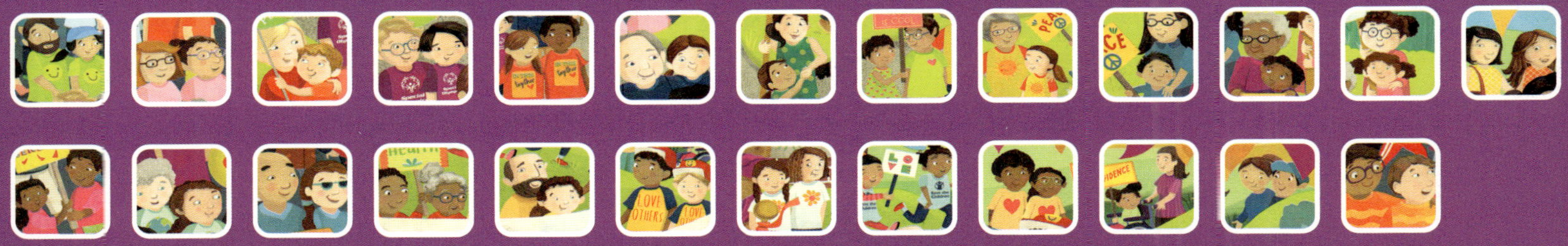

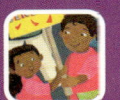

MAKING A DIFFERENCE

My name is ....

My buddy's name is ....

Together we will ....

Draw a picture of you and your buddy working to make a positive difference.

**SMITH PUBLICITY, INC.
FOR REVIEW ONLY
RESALE PROHIBITED**
Excluding Nonprofit Organizations